The Sioux

ANNA REBUS

Weigl

CALGARY

www.weigl.com

Published by Weigl Educational Publishers Limited
6325 10 Street SE
Calgary, Alberta, Canada
T2H 2Z9

Website: www.weigl.com

Library and Archives Canada Cataloguing in Publication data available upon request.
Fax (403) 233-7769 for the attention of the Publishing Records department.

ISBN 978-1-55388-426-2 (hard cover)
ISBN 978-1-55388-427-9 (soft cover)

Printed in the United States of America
1 2 3 4 5 6 7 8 9 0 12 11 10 09 08

Project Coordinator Heather Kissock **Design** Janine Vangool **Layout** Terry Paulhus
Validator Susana D. Geliga

Photograph credits
Every reasonable effort has been made to trace ownership and to obtain permission to reprint copyright material. The publishers would be pleased to have any errors or omissions brought to their attention so that they may be corrected in subsequent printings.

Cover: Canadian Museum of Civilization (V-E-24, D2004-25129 - main), Alamy (top left), Getty Images (top centre), Canadian Museum of Civilization (V-E-164, D2005-21019 - top right); **Alamy:** pages 6, 14T, 18, 19, 20, 21, 24; **All Canada Photos:** page 27; **Canadian Museum of Civilization:** pages 14M (V-E-201,D2004-25427), 14B (V-C-221, D2004-25450), 15T (V-E-136, D2004-26826), 15B (V-E-67, D2004-25189), 25L (V-E-124, D2004-25170), 25R (V-E-24, D2004-25129), 28T (V-E-358, D2004-27571), 28B (V-E-340, D2004-25240), 29 (V-E-164, D2005-21019), 30 (V-E-24, D2004-25129); **Corbis:** pages 5, 9, 10, 11L, 11R, 15M, 22, 23, 26; **Getty Images:** pages 1, 3, 7, 8, 13, 16, 17.

We acknowledge the financial support of the Government of Canada through the Book Publishing Industry Development Program (BPIDP) for our publishing activities.

Please note
All of the Internet URLs given in the book were valid at the time of publication. However, due to the dynamic nature of the Internet, some addresses may have changed, or sites may have ceased to exist since publication. While the author and publisher regret any inconvenience this may cause readers, no responsibility for any such changes can be accepted by either the author or the publisher.

CONTENTS

The People

The Sioux are one of many **First Nations** groups that lived on the **Interior Plains** of North America. The Sioux did not always live in this area. **Archaeologists** have found evidence that the Sioux lived in what is now western Ontario and eastern Manitoba before spreading south into present-day Wisconsin and Minnesota in the United States. It is here that European explorers first met the Sioux.

Europeans introduced the Sioux to the horse. This animal helped the Sioux expand their territory. In the early 1700s, the Sioux began moving south and west toward the Prairies, settling in parts of present-day Manitoba, Saskatchewan, and Alberta as well as the present-day states of Wyoming, Montana, and North and South Dakota.

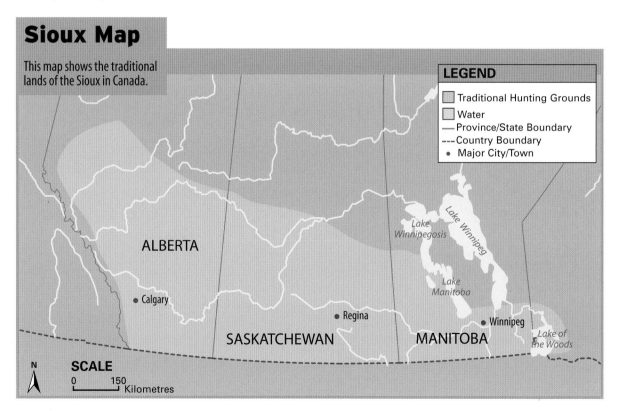

Sioux Map

This map shows the traditional lands of the Sioux in Canada.

LEGEND
- Traditional Hunting Grounds
- Water
- —— Province/State Boundary
- --- Country Boundary
- • Major City/Town

ALBERTA

SASKATCHEWAN

MANITOBA

• Calgary

• Regina

• Winnipeg

Lake Winnipegosis

Lake Winnipeg

Lake Manitoba

Lake of the Woods

N

SCALE
0   150
Kilometres

Over time, three different language **dialects**, Dakota, Lakota, and Nakota, emerged among the Sioux. All of these words mean "allies," or "friends." Together, the Dakota, Lakota, and Nakota groups are known as the Great Sioux Nation.

In the past, the Sioux moved from place to place, following bison herds as they moved with the seasons. Today, many Sioux live in towns and cities. Others live on **reserves** in Canada and the United States.

The Sioux have not forgotten their traditional way of life. Many work hard to pass on stories, dances, crafts, and customs to their children.

On specific occasions, the Sioux wear their traditional regalia. This is one way they honour their history.

Many Sioux in Canada do not have the same rights as other First Nations groups. This is because the Canadian government feels that the Sioux are not truly Canadian. Instead, the government believes that the Sioux are **refugees** from the United States.

In 1862, a battle broke out in the United States due to the European expansion. The military drove many Sioux, especially the Dakotas, off their lands and into Canada. Some of these Sioux decided to stay in Canada, where they settled on reserves.

The Canadian government set aside reserve land for these Sioux, but it did not grant all of them **treaty status**. This meant that they could not claim traditional lands for themselves, as many other Canadian First Nations are able to do. They also do not have the same rights as First Nations groups that have treaty status.

Still, Canada's Sioux have been able to create lives for themselves. They can be found working in towns, cities, and other communities.

Sioux Homes

Traditionally, the Sioux lived in teepees. A teepee was made with bison hides and tree poles. The long tree poles were leaned against each other and tied at the top to make a cone shape. Bison hides were stretched over the poles. The Sioux needed homes that would suit their way of life. Teepees were easy to build and move. They allowed the Sioux to move from place to place as they followed the bison herds.

In the summer months, the teepee hides could be rolled up to allow fresh air inside. All teepees had a small doorway opening that was covered with a bison hide. Wood or bone pins held the doorway in place.

Teepees were so easy to construct and dismantle that they could be taken down and packed within 30 minutes.

DWELLING AND DECORATION

In the centre of the teepee, the Sioux built a hearth, or fire pit, for cooking and heating. Two flaps at the top of the teepee opened to release smoke from the hearth. The flaps could also be closed to keep out rain, snow, or wind. Stones and wooden stakes held down the bottom of the teepee.

Sioux women played a key role in making the teepees. They prepared bison hides in a process known as tanning. First, the women stretched the hides and scraped them clean using tools made from bones or elk antlers. They then soaked the hides in water for several days. Afterward, they rubbed animal fats and animal brains into the hides to make them soft. They washed and softened the hides once more. Finally, the hides were smoked over a low fire to make them waterproof.

When built properly, a teepee is strong enough to withstand very high winds.

Sioux Communities

Traditional Sioux communities were built around family members and relatives. Each generation was taught to respect its elders. Everyone was taught to live in harmony with one another and with nature.

The Sioux's survival depended on everyone doing his or her job. Sioux men had many different jobs. The chief was a well-respected man who represented his people at important events, such as treaty signings. Other men were hunters, while some were scouts who went searching for bison and other wild animals. These men worked together to find meat and hides. The warriors helped keep everyone safe. There were also storytellers who told tales to remind communities about history and religious beliefs.

Even though the Sioux moved often, each community remained united at all times. Its members travelled and settled together.

Men performed specific tasks as part of their daily lives. The skills they displayed in these tasks earned them respect within the community. They were recognized for their healing powers, hunting skills, courage as warriors, wisdom in settling arguments, or skill in trade with other **Aboriginal** groups.

Women had specific roles within the community as well. They took care of the children, prepared food, collected firewood, made clothing, and built teepees. Sometimes, they led ceremonies. Women owned the teepees and everything inside them. They were respected because they were givers of life.

In the past, Sioux children did not attend school. Every day, they learned valuable lessons and skills from family members. Girls learned to tan hides and cook food, while boys learned to hunt using bows and arrows.

Most parents arranged marriages for their children. During the marriage ceremony, the families of the bride and groom exchanged gifts as a sign of friendship and respect.

Children were respected members of the community. They were believed to have come from the spiritual world.

Sioux Clothing

In the past, the Sioux had two types of clothing. One type was worn for daily tasks. The other was worn for special occasions or ceremonies.

The Sioux made their clothing from tanned deer or elk hides. Women wore knee-length dresses. They also wore leggings that reached to the knee. Men wore sleeveless shirts and breechcloths, which are similar to short pants. In the winter, men wore leggings and bison robes.

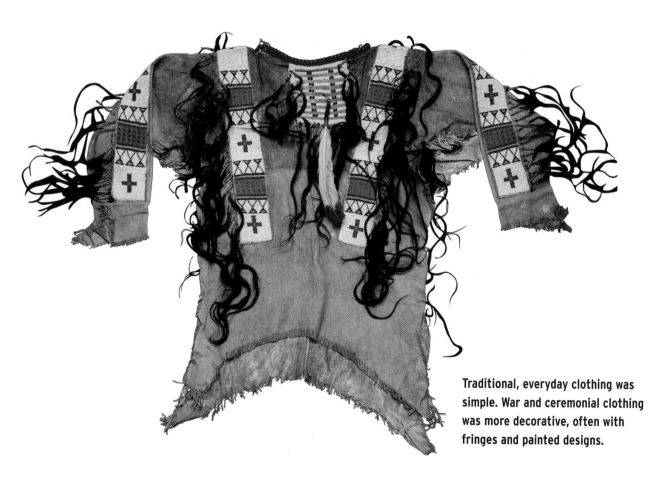

Traditional, everyday clothing was simple. War and ceremonial clothing was more decorative, often with fringes and painted designs.

Sioux men and women had many different ways to decorate their clothing. They often wore jewellery, such as colourful bone necklaces and armbands, which were decorated with beads. Women used their knowledge of making dyes to paint or tattoo designs on their faces and bodies. Warriors and hunters painted their faces and the halters of their horses with bright colours. The beautiful designs they painted were thought to encourage the support of important spirits.

The Sioux wore animal hide shoes called moccasins. Moccasins were often decorated with colourful quillwork or beadwork. Each community had its own style of decoration.

In the past, the Sioux would sometimes decorate their bodies for religious reasons. Sioux men believed that wearing a single eagle feather gave them the bird's strength and bravery. They also believed the Great Spirit would help and protect them when they wore an eagle feather. The feather could be worn in their hair or as part of a headdress.

Headdresses made of many feathers were worn only on special occasions, such as during treaty meetings. Today, the headdress is still considered special. It is worn at events such as tribal meetings and **wacipi**.

Sioux beadwork normally featured geometric patterns, such as triangles and diamonds.

Sioux Food

At one time, millions of bison roamed the Interior Plains. Bison was the Sioux's most important food source. The Sioux boiled bison meat with wild vegetables, such as turnips or onions. They added wild berries for extra flavour. Sometimes, they roasted the meat on a stick over a fire or cut it into strips and placed it on racks to dry. Dried meat would not spoil for a long time. Sioux men also hunted antelope, deer, and elk for food.

It was difficult to find food during the winter. Sioux men hunted bison in the summer and fall. Many Aboriginal Peoples, including the Sioux, made pemmican. Pemmican was made of dried meat that was pounded into powder and mixed with melted animal fat and berries. The Sioux ate pemmican during the long winter because it would not spoil.

European settlers also brought many food items to the Sioux. The Sioux learned to use these new ingredients, such as flour, sugar, baking soda, seasonings, and coffee, along with their traditional food.

The Sioux created fry bread when they were moved to reserves and rationed on foods such as flour, lard, and salt.

Sioux Fry Bread

Ingredients:

574 millilitres flour

15 mL baking powder

5 mL salt

237 mL milk

oil for frying

Equipment:

large bowl

wooden spoon

frying pan, deep fryer, or wok

slotted spoon

sifter

Directions

1. Sift flour and baking powder together in a bowl.

2. Slowly stir in milk. Add more flour as necessary to make the dough less sticky.

3. Coat your hands and the tabletop with flour.

4. Knead the dough until it is smooth. The dough should not stick to your finger when poked.

5. Preheat the oil to about 191° Celsius in a frying pan, deep fryer, or wok.

6. With an adult's help, place one or two teaspoon-size portions of dough in the hot oil.

7. Cook the dough on both sides until golden brown. This should take about 5 minutes.

8. Use a slotted spoon to remove the cooked dough from the oil. Drain on a paper towel.

Tools, Weapons, and Defence

Before Europeans arrived, the Sioux made tools from stone, bone, and wood. By carefully selecting stones and chipping away at them, the Sioux made stone knives, scrapers, and arrowheads.

The Sioux also used parts of the bison to make tools. Knives, scrapers, drills, and needles were made from bison bones. Cups and bowls were made from bison horns, while bags and containers were made from bison organs.

Before the Sioux had horses, they used dogs as pack animals. The Sioux attached two poles to the dog's shoulders to form an A-shaped frame. The poles dragged on the ground, and skins held them together. This device was called a travois. Belongings that needed to be transported were piled on the skins. When the Sioux began using horses, they created larger travois that could carry more belongings.

Teepee poles were used to make the travois.

Large stones or rocks often were used as hammers.

Skin scrapers were used to clean buffalo hides.

WAR AND HUNTING

The Sioux were excellent hunters and brave warriors. They used lances, or spears, and bows and arrows to hunt bison and other wild animals. These hunting weapons were also used as weapons of war.

Before guns arrived on the Prairies, the bow and arrow was the main weapon used by the Sioux. To make bows, willow branches were boiled, shaped, and dried into a near half-circle shape. The Sioux made arrowheads from rocks that had been carefully chipped and shaped to a point. Sinew, a tough tissue that connects muscles to bones, connected the arrowhead to a willow branch shaft. Feathers were attached to the end of the willow shaft to help it fly straight. An animal hide grip allowed the warrior or hunter to hold the bow tightly while aiming the arrow.

The Sioux and other Interior Plains Aboriginal groups used shields made from animal hides. Symbols decorated the shields. The Sioux believed these symbols would help protect a warrior in battle.

Europeans introduced new weapons, including guns, to the Sioux. Guns and swift horses helped make the Sioux fearless warriors. Guns also made it easier for the Sioux to hunt bison.

The Sioux normally used spears when they were riding horses.

Bison hide was also used to construct quivers, which are containers that hold arrows.

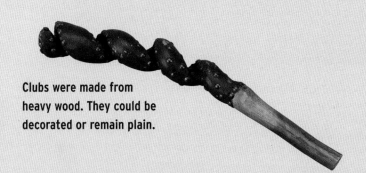

Clubs were made from heavy wood. They could be decorated or remain plain.

Sioux Religion

Religion was an important part of the Sioux's everyday life. The Sioux believed every living thing had a spirit. All creatures and things on Earth were connected and depended on one another.

Wakan Tanka, or the Great Spirit, was the most important spirit. The Sioux believed the Great Spirit existed at the beginning of time and created all living things. The Great Spirit also created the Sun, the Moon, and the stars.

The Sioux believed a medicine person could communicate with the spirit world. Since the Sioux believed spirits caused illness, the medicine person was also a healer.

Each community had at least one medicine man or woman. The Sioux believed that medicine men and women were either born with the ability to communicate with spirits or learned it at an early age. Medicine men and women were highly respected in the community because the Sioux believed they had the power to control spirits and cure illnesses.

Today, medicine men and women continue to heal people in Sioux communities using traditional medicines. Medicine men and women are still respected for their knowledge and wisdom.

Medicine men and women remain an important part of Sioux society. They offer prayers to the spirit world on behalf of the community.

Ceremonies and Celebrations

The Sioux performed many rituals, religious ceremonies, and celebrations. At these events, men and women performed songs and special dances.

One of the main outlets for this type of celebration was wacipi, which some First Nations groups call a powwow. These events still take place today. The main focus of wacipi is social. People have an opportunity to talk with old friends and make new ones.

Dancing, singing, and drumming are key parts of wacipi and bring **spirituality** to the event. To the Sioux, the beat of the drum represents the heartbeat of Earth. The circle of life is represented in the dancing area. By dancing in this area, the dancers are expressing their understanding of the role they play in this circle.

Each year, wacipi celebrations are held between March and September. Wacipi include singing, dancing, and visiting with friends and family.

Another religious practice that Sioux boys, and sometimes girls, participated in as they matured was a **vision quest**. A vision quest lasted four days. The young person travelled to a distant place and prayed for a vision of a spirit. This spirit became the boy's or girl's guardian.

A vision quest helps young Sioux find their path in life.

SWEAT LODGE

The sweat lodge was an important part of Sioux life. It was a place for the Sioux to cleanse and heal themselves. They entered the sweat lodge to reflect on the personal issues facing them.

A sweat lodge was built using trees and twigs which were bent into a dome or teepee shape. A fire pit containing heated rocks was placed in the centre of the lodge. Water poured over the rocks produced the steam to heat the structure.

To the Sioux, the interior of the lodge represented the womb of Mother Earth. So, entering the lodge was a time to connect with one's spirituality. The entrance to a Sioux sweat lodge almost always faced east, as this was seen as the direction from which life, power, and wisdom was believed to originate. The Sioux continue to seek guidance in sweat lodges to this day.

Music and Dance

Music has always been an important part of Sioux life. The Sioux have a rich catalogue of songs. Some songs have been developed for performances and social occasions. These are called traditional songs. Ceremonial songs are used only during specific ceremonies. Songs have been specially created for sweat lodge and pipe lighting ceremonies.

Two of the most common traditional Sioux songs are the flag song and the honour song. The flag song is played at the beginning of wacipi. It is similar to a national anthem and celebrates the Sioux's loyalty to Canada and its monarch. When the flag song is played, everyone is expected to stand and take off their headgear. There is no dancing while the flag song is being performed.

Honour songs are performed to pay respect to a member of the Sioux community. They can be performed to celebrate birthdays, anniversaries, or other special occasions. Honour songs may be specially composed for the person or be a standard song that is adapted for the person being honoured. The song is often accompanied by dancing.

Sioux of all ages participate in ceremonial dancing.

CEREMONIAL DANCING

The Sioux have many different dances that they perform. One dance the Sioux perform at a wacipi is the Jingle Dress Dance. This traditional dance was created in the 1920s. Dancers wear clothing with detailed beadwork and feathers. Their dresses are also covered with hundreds of small metal cones. As the dancers move to the beat of the music, the metal cones jingle. Men and women, young and old, take part in the dances. As was customary long ago, people attending wacipi today must be respectful and considerate of one another.

The hoop dance is popular among the Sioux. To them, hoops represent the never-ending circle of life.

Language and Storytelling

The Dakota, Lakota, and Nakota Sioux speak different dialects of the same language. This means that the words themselves or the organization of words are similar, but the pronunciation or spelling may be different. For example, the Dakota word for "thank you" is *pidamiye*. The Lakota word for "thank you" is *pilamiye*. The Nakota word for "thank you" is *pinamiye*.

By studying the Sioux language and its dialects, it is possible to understand how the Dakota, Lakota, and Nakota people and their languages are related. The dialects also help to show how the Sioux language changed over time.

Stories and traditions are passed on by Sioux storytellers or chanters.

In the past, the Sioux did not have a written alphabet. They passed on their history in a number of ways, including painting images on bison hides, painting or carving pictures into rocks, and telling stories. Storytelling was used to teach and entertain. Elders often gathered the young people around a fire to tell stories and legends. Children listened and were taught proper behaviour, traditional customs, and family history. To test their memory, children might be asked to repeat the stories, some of which may have taken several evenings to tell.

The Sioux also used sign language to communicate. Sign language uses hand gestures and movement to express actions and ideas. Sign language was very useful for communicating with members from other Sioux communities who spoke different dialects and languages.

Stories could be told orally or through paintings on robes or other pieces of clothing.

Sioux Art

The Sioux used materials they found in nature to decorate everyday items and create art. They made dyes out of plants or minerals. They also made beads from porcupine quills and seeds.

The Sioux passed their history on through stories and painted images. Sioux historians painted important events on a piece of hide, which was called a winter count. The historians passed on the meaning of the painted pictures so that no one would forget what they meant.

The pictures on a winter count could be quite detailed and elaborate.

Before the Sioux began living on the Interior Plains, they lived in an area that covered present-day Minnesota, Wisconsin, western Ontario, and eastern Manitoba. Here, they made pottery containers, which they used for cooking and storage. However, as the Sioux moved farther west, pottery became too heavy to carry long distances. The Sioux began using **parfleches** to store things because they were light and easy to carry. They often decorated parfleches with detailed and beautiful designs.

Today, many Sioux earn an income as artists. Some Sioux artists create paintings, sculptures, bronzes, or photographs to express themselves and to teach people about their culture and way of life.

Decoration added colour to moccasins, clothing, and ceremonial objects. Women spent many hours creating quill and beadwork designs on scraped and prepared animal hides. Women often decorated hides with thin, hollow porcupine quills. They pulled quills from the dead animal, organized them by size, and dyed the quills different colours. Quills could be up to 10 centimetres long. Each community had its own style of decoration and design. Certain colours or shapes, such as triangles or rectangles, might be more important to one community than to another. When European traders arrived, Sioux women began using glass beads in their work. The Sioux valued glass beads because they did not require preparation, came in brilliant colours, and sparkled in the sunlight.

Parfleches often were used to store food or clothing.

Star Quilts

The morning star has been an important Sioux symbol for a very long time. It was painted onto teepees, battle shields, bison robes, and other clothing long before Europeans arrived in the area. To the Sioux, the morning star represented the journey from darkness, or ignorance, to light, or knowledge.

When European **missionaries** arrived in the area, they brought new sewing techniques and materials with them. One of these techniques was quilting, in which a type of blanket is made by sewing pieces of material together into patterns.

Sioux women quickly learned to quilt and began making different types of patterns. The most popular pattern, however, was the star. These star quilts served as gifts for many different occasions, from birthdays to weddings.

Today, Sioux women continue to make star quilts. They are considered to be one of the most valued gifts the Sioux can give someone. It is considered an honour to receive one.

Sioux star quilts are known for their unique and creative use of colour.

MODERN ARTIST

Maxine Noel

Maxine Noel is a Sioux artist who is known for working in a variety of media, from painting to needlework. She was born on the Birdtail Reservation in southwest Manitoba in 1946 and was the eldest of eleven children. Maxine lived under the nurture of her parents until she was six years old. She then, like many Aboriginal children at the time, was sent to a **residential school** for her education.

Even before entering school, Maxine loved to draw. This joy continued into adulthood, although she did not immediately explore a career in art. Following school, she became a legal secretary, working in Edmonton and Toronto. She continued developing her artistic skills while she worked her day-job.

While working at an Aboriginal friendship centre in northern Ontario, a friend encouraged her to show her artwork to a Toronto art dealer. The art dealer was impressed and quickly planned an exhibition. It was held in 1980 at the Thomson Gallery in Ontario. From that point on, Maxine's reputation as an artist grew, and more exhibitions were held in Canada and the United States. Her work now has an international following.

Maxine's work is known for its fluidity and its use of subtle colours. Critics have commented that her flowing style gives an impression of serene strength to her subjects. Maxine's paintings also feature a high level of **abstraction**, which contributes to their uniqueness.

Maxine continues to grow as an artist. Besides painting, she has also expanded her artistic range to include etching and lithography. In 2002, she was awarded the Golden Jubilee Medal by Queen Elizabeth for her outstanding service to Canada. Maxine now lives in Stratford, Ontario.

Stratford, Ontario is a picturesque town best known for its annual theatre festival devoted to the plays of William Shakespeare.

Studying the Past

Archaeologists study items left by people from the past. The Sioux left many **artifacts** behind. From these artifacts, archaeologists can learn more about how the Sioux lived.

Scientists have discovered that, before the Europeans brought metal cooking pots to the Interior Plains, the Sioux cooked foods, such as stew, in bison stomachs. They heated rocks in a fire and then placed the rocks in the stew. The heat from the rocks cooked the stew. If the rocks were heated and cooled many times, they broke. These rocks are called fire broken rock.

Archaeologists have also found stone circles called teepee rings on the Prairies. These stones helped hold down the base of the teepee. When the Sioux moved to a new location, they packed up their teepees and left the stones behind.

Archaeologists have found Sioux artifacts, such as stone and bone tools, arrowheads, and hearths, too.

Artifacts, such as clubs and rattles, help archaeologists form a picture of what made up traditional Sioux life.

TIMELINE

Prior to 1200 AD

Archaeological evidence indicates that the Sioux occupied parts of present-day Manitoba, eastern Saskatchewan, and western Ontario.

1200 to 1680

The Sioux move south to what are now the U.S. states of Wisconsin and Minnesota. Pierre Radisson, a French explorer, makes first contact with the Sioux in 1659.

Around 1680

The Sioux move to what is now eastern North and South Dakota.

Late 1700s

The Sioux now live in the Dakotas, Wyoming, and eastern Montana. Europeans introduce horses to the Sioux. As a result, the Sioux expand their territory into Canada, from present-day Saskatchewan to Ontario.

1812

The Sioux pledge their allegiance to Great Britain during the War of 1812.

1814

At the end of the war, Britain does not honour its commitment to the Sioux. The Sioux return to their U.S. lands.

1862–1864

The U.S. military drives many Dakota Sioux into Canada in order to assist with European settlement. Some Dakota eventually move back to the U.S., while others remain and settle in Canada.

1870s

The Canadian government refuses to sign a treaty with the Dakota Sioux. It says that the Dakota are refugees to Canada and not Canadian citizens. Nakota Sioux in Saskatchewan and Alberta are given treaty status.

2006

The Dakota Sioux issue a land claim for parts of Manitoba.

2007

The Canadian government rejects the Dakota Sioux's claims to traditional lands.

The Sioux carried the materials they needed to make fire in a decorated container called a fire bag.

Make Your Own Parfleche Bag

Parfleches were rawhide containers. The Sioux used them to hold food, clothing, and other items. They were decorated with colourful designs. Parfleches were light and easy to carry. You can make your own parfleche container. While this parfleche will not be made of rawhide, it will give you a good idea how a parfleche was created and decorated. Your parfleche will be folded much like a large envelope.

You will need:

- One piece of 28-cm by 43-cm beige or light brown construction paper
- One 30-cm piece of leather or regular string
- Felt markers or crayons
- Scissors
- Hole punch
- 4 reinforcements

Steps

1. Use the diagram below as a guide for cutting the construction paper into the shape of the parfleche bag.
2. Cut along the dark lines to remove a 5 cm by 10 cm section of each corner of the paper.
3. Using a hole punch, punch out two holes on the C flaps, near the edge of the paper. The string will be threaded through these holes.
4. Along the dotted line, fold the A flaps toward each other.
5. Along the dotted line, fold the B flaps toward the C flaps.
6. Fold the C flaps toward and on top of the A flaps.
7. Loop the string through the holes and tie by making a bow. You may need to use reinforcements on the holes to prevent the paper from tearing.
8. Plains Indians would often decorate the outside of flaps A or C in colorful geometric designs. Decorate your parfleche using felt markers or crayons.

	A	
B		B
C		C
1" B		B
2" A		

4"

FURTHER READING

Further Reading

Moonstick: The Seasons of the Sioux by Eve Bunting (Harper Collins Canada, 2000) recounts the story of a boy who learns a Sioux tradition and much more from his father.

The background and impact of the Sioux's movement between Canada and the United States in the 1800s is examined in David McCrady's *Living with Strangers: The Nineteenth-Century Sioux and the Canadian-American Borderlands* (University of Nebraska, 2006).

Websites

Learn more about Canada's Sioux at **esask.uregina.ca/entry/ dakota__lakota.html**.

A biography about Maxine Noel can be found at **www.ourheirlooms.com/ artists/maxine-noel.shtml**.

Read different Sioux Indian legends at **www.indianlegend.com/sioux/ sioux_index.htm**

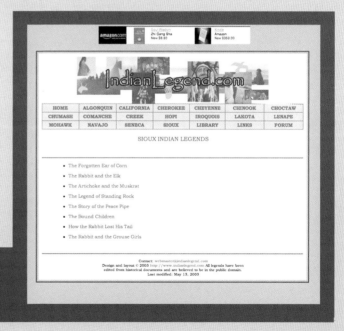

GLOSSARY

Aboriginal: the original or earliest inhabitants of a place

abstraction: having to do with a style of art that does not show real objects, but uses lines, shapes, and colours to suggest an idea or feeling

archaeologists: scientists who study objects from the past to learn about people who lived long ago

artifacts: objects used or made by humans long ago

dialects: changes in a language that is spoken from place to place

First Nations: members of Canada's Aboriginal community who are not Inuit or Métis

Interior Plains: the rolling, low-lying land found in central Canada; sometimes called the Prairies

missionaries: people who teach others about Christianity

parfleches: animal hide containers

refugees: people who have had to move from one country to another as a result of war

reserves: areas of land set aside for First Nations to live on if they choose

residential school: a boarding school for Aboriginal students set up by the federal government

spirituality: experiencing sacred or religious thought

treaty status: protected by the rights of a treaty, or an agreement between two nations

vision quest: a time to pray and seek guidance

wacipi: a dance festival involving singing, dancing, and drumming

INDEX